The Light of Home

Ten Inspiring Pictures of a Strong Family

Dr. John Trent
paintings by
Thomas Kinkade

HARVEST HOUSE™ PUBLISHERS

EUGENE, OREGON

The *Light of Home*

Text Copyright © 2002 by John Trent, Ph.D.
Published by Harvest House Publishers
Eugene, Oregon 97402

Library of Congress Cataloging-in-Publication Data
Trent, John T.
    The light of home / John Trent ; paintings by Thomas Kinkade.
        p. cm.
Includes bibliographical references (p.   ).
    ISBN 0-7369-1017-4
    1. Family—Religious life. 2. Family—Religious
aspects—Christianity. I. Title.
    BV4526.2 .T75 2002

                                        2002003157

Design and production by Koechel Peterson & Associates, Minneapolis, Minnesota

Published in association with the literary agency of Alive Communications, Inc., 7680 Goddard
Street, Suite 200, Colorado Springs, CO 80920.

The Light of Home

Ten Inspiring Pictures of a Strong Family

STRONG FAMILIES

Strong families are the heart of a strong nation, and no one knows this better than John Trent. The first chapter in this remarkable volume is titled, "Now, More Than Ever." There is something prophetic about this construction. For John, pondering the needs of the American family predates any of the current circumstances of world affairs. In fact, John has long realized that the family is more than just the building block of society; it is the very sanctuary where the human soul can thrive and grow.

Like the pioneers of another century who gathered their families together for a westward trek across the prairies, John sees our families as voyagers in the journey of life. And, like the pioneers who would circle their wagons in the evening for protection, today's pioneers in family living must circle around foundational values if families are to survive.

It should be obvious to any citizen of the twenty-first century that the darkness of our world— the hatred, suffering, and evil—seems more threatening than ever before. And yet staving off this darkness is the simple light of human love and compassion. It is this light of love, more than any other message, that enlivens these practical lessons for building a strong family. If each family can kindle this light anew in the coming years, our entire nation, and perhaps the entire world, may someday be warmed by its glow.

Thomas Kinkade
CARMEL, CALIFORNIA

CONTENTS

NOW, MORE
THAN EVER

It was during the tragedy, sadness, and terrible loss of life that marked our American Civil War that President Abraham Lincoln observed, "The strength of our country lies in the homes of our people." That is absolutely true today. Our world was rocked by the acts of terror that began on September 11, 2001, and ever since then our view of what's most important has changed dramatically. In particular, Americans have awoken once again to how important strong families are in stressful times.

It's still hard for many Americans to believe, but we are now at war with a host of determined enemies. And though these terrorists who hate our way of life operate in darkness, their goals have nothing to do with subtlety and shadow. When terrorists strike, their acts of hatred are carefully planned so they can be seen in the brightest light. Their strategy is to fill our eyes—and then our hearts—with pictures of fear. And it is from these terrible pictures that they hope to destroy our resolve and strike fear into our hearts.

TERRORISTS' PICTURES ARE MEANT TO MAKE US LOSE HEART

Listen to these penetrating words on the manipulative power that terrorists seek to wield in our lives:

A hundred petty crimes or petty accidents will not strike the imagination of crowds in the least, whereas a single great crime or a single great accident will profoundly impress them, even though the results be infinitely less disastrous than the hundreds of small accidents put together.

The epidemic of influenza, which caused the death of five thousand persons in Paris alone a few years ago, made very little impression on the popular imagination. Yet an accident causing the death of only five hundred persons, but all on the same day and in public, as the outcome of the fall, for instance, of the Eiffel Tower, would have produced, on the contrary, an immense impression on the imagination of the crowd.[1]

These aren't the words of an Al Qaeda operative or Osama bin Laden himself. They were written by Frenchman Gustave le Bon *115 years ago!*

His book *The Crowd—A Study of the Popular Mind* has been called a "timeless handbook" on how to manipulate and brainwash people. In fact, it matches nearly line for line the tactics employed by today's terrorists and the pictures they want to paint in people's minds.

As if to prove le Bon's point, more than 35,000 people are killed each year on our nation's highways. More than 300,000 die each year from lung and throat cancer caused by smoking cigarettes. Yet these individual losses,  spread out by geography and occurring incrementally, do not bring the collective sense of loss that comes with a single great tragedy.

Far from being unschooled or unsophisticated, terrorists understand the "picture power" that a major disaster has on the public's imagination. They know the words "This news just breaking!" mean that *every* major network will immediately begin broadcasting as much live audio and video footage from the scene as possible. They count on replays of a horrific event

and endless commentary by political pundits and quickly-called "experts."

With pictures of catastrophe, terrorists seek to demoralize and ultimately defeat us by plunging our country into panic, withdrawal, and inaction. Note the words of Osama bin Laden in his first video broadcast after the World Trade Center bombing: "America is full of fear from its north to its south, from its west to its east. Thank God for that."

To be certain, seeing the Pentagon awash in flames and suffocating clouds of dust swallowing up streets and people fleeing from the falling World Trade Center Towers left an unnerving and unforgettable image. *But though these terrible pictures have the power to shock and sadden us, they must not define us.*

In fact, it is how we *react* to the pictures we've been handed—and we will be handed more terrible pictures in the future—that will prove to be the challenge of our times and of each American family.

THE PICTURES WE MUST PRESERVE

Exactly one month to the day after the World Trade Center Towers collapsed, at a podium near the still-smoldering ruins, New York Mayor Rudolph Giuliani addressed police officers, firefighters, rescue personnel, and construction workers. Speaking to these heroes—and to the rest of us—the mayor urged all Americans to see beyond the terrible pictures.

"Look at the determination you see around you. Don't look at these ruins. Look at the resolve filling our great city and nation. Don't look at the shock of the moment, but the strength that has come from this terrible event."

Mayor Giuliani was absolutely right. The way out of the fear and confusion so many still feel won't be found in watching slow-motion replays of kidnapped planes being swallowed up by twin 110-story buildings. Nor will you find the fate of our nation lying in the tons of twisted steel and pulverized concrete left behind at the Pentagon.

In fearful, troubling times like these, I'm convinced our eyes need to turn to pictures that highlight the best of our nation.

We can take comfort in the paintings and photographs of historical events from America's past that  show us the courage and resolve other Americans displayed in times of adversity. Pictures like Emanuel Leutze's painting of General George Washington crossing the Delaware River. This revered painting of courage captures a freezing night when Washington and his victory-starved army surprised the British and Hessian troops on the day after Christmas in 1776. Or photographs like the hurried snapshot of a handful of Marines raising a flag over Iwo Jima as the battle raged below—an enduring image of American heroism replicated when New York City firefighters raised a flag in the midst of the World Trade Center rubble.

Yet, perhaps in a surprising way, it is not the pictures of battle, but the pictures of enduring American beauty—and especially pictures of home—that may be the greatest help in healing our wounds and giving us strength of heart.

IN TRYING TIMES, WE NEED TO CONCENTRATE ON THE RIGHT PICTURES

Our deepest passions of patriotism, family, and faith are awakened by pictures of stunning American landscapes, of hearth and loving home, of families walking together on a winter night, and of simpler times in our country's history.

In times of great trial and loss, we've known this truth instinctively. Soldiers, sailors, airmen, and Marines caught up in a foreign war have drawn on these pictures of America to sustain them through battle. For the Navajo code talkers in World War II, it was the longing to see the sun setting over a red-hued Arizona desert mesa. For a Vietnam veteran surrounded for 13 months by a triple-canopy green jungle, it was the memory of fall leaves of Upper Michigan turning dazzling shades of wine-colored

WE CAN TAKE COMFORT IN . . .

HISTORICAL EVENTS FROM AMERICA'S PAST THAT SHOW US THE COURAGE AND RESOLVE OTHER AMERICANS DISPLAYED IN TIMES OF ADVERSITY.

burgundies mingled with saffron, honey, and gold. For a Desert Storm soldier staring at countless waves of sand dunes, it was the longing to see rows of narrow, red-brick houses lining a rain-slick Chicago street.

Today, it's the sailor or airman or woman on the flight deck of a carrier in the Persian Gulf longing to see fields being planted; or for a Marine looking up at the mountains of Afganistan, it's remembering a family trip to Colorado as a child.

As one combat veteran poignantly observed, being constantly surrounded by terrible pictures during wartime exchanges one kind of "normal" for another. "In war you learn survival skills to fit an extreme situation, but in the long run they are not life skills. So if a GI is ever to go back to a 'normal' life, he needs to hear about the church bake sale, who won the big high school football game, and what clever trick the family dog has learned."

Now, with the battle being carried to our shores, it's as if each American has awoken in a war zone. In order to get back to some kind of a "new normal," I'm convinced that it will be the everyday things—the everyday pictures of America—that will renew our resolve and restore to us a sense of reality.

These commonplace pictures challenge us to make the necessary sacrifices so that our country and freedoms will be safe for future generations. And these are the pictures of America that I feel are captured so powerfully in the works of the great contemporary American artist, Thomas Kinkade.

As you turn the pages of this book, you'll find his inspiring art capturing hearth-warmed homes, warmly lit windows, and the majesty of God displayed in various American cities and landscapes. Thomas Kinkade, who is best known as the beloved "Painter of Light," has given us hundreds of paintings over the years. He is a national treasure, and I am honored to call him my friend.

Thomas Kinkade has shown us through his masterful use of color and light on canvas the truths we'll explore more deeply in the pages that follow. In particular, we'll see in these words what you see in his paintings—that the darker it gets on the outside, the more we need our homes to light up from the inside.

What follows in words and art are ten positive "pictures"—ten principles that can specifically show you how to have a home full of light. Each chapter is a reflection or a principle or a truth that American families in each generation tried in their most difficult, darkest hours and found to be true.

As you turn each page, it's our hope that two things will take place in your heart. We pray that each of these ten images and ideas will not only help you experience the title of this book—*The Light of Home*—but will help you live up to a Presidential Proclamation issued less than two weeks after the terrorist attacks.

On September 24, 2001, President George W. Bush issued a stirring proclamation for the families of America which began with these words:

Strong families make a strong America.

Our president's words remind us that the way to move forward in times of great trial and pain is to draw together with our loved ones. When it comes to homeland defense, *we can fight back each day against the enemies of our freedoms by drawing closer to our family.* Some will be called on to serve in foreign and domestic battles in the days to come. But every American can learn more about living out the words "strong families make a strong America."

For now, more than ever, we need such encouragement.

Now, more than ever, we need to live courageous, caring, meaningful lives.

And now, more than ever...*our country needs strong families.*

The First Picture

Facing Up to Our Past Mistakes & Moving On

 recently ran across some amazing information on New Year's resolutions that shows just how much people's goals have changed as a result of what's happened to our country.

For decades, pollsters have contacted people on New Year's Eve and asked them the question: "What is your number one New Year's resolution this year?" Most polling centers, including the Gallup Organization, have conducted yearly surveys and found that the most often heard response is always the same. Can you guess what it would be?

That's right: "I'm going to lose weight this year!"

But after 9/11, not only did our world change, but so did the number one New Year's resolution. On December 31, 2001, the top vote getter wasn't to lose weight. It was:

"I want to have a closer family."

That's a wonderful resolution, and it's tremendous that in our country, at least on the day this poll was taken, we were more concerned with the loved ones we hold dear than the pounds we hold near. But how do we keep this truly laudable goal of having a stronger family from the usual fate of all our *other* New Year's resolutions? In other words, how can we keep our goal of growing closer to others from evaporating as quickly as our promise to "never eat another donut" or to "exercise every day"?

How can we have a strong family in these stressful times—starting today?

Let me suggest that for most people, the first step forward begins by taking one step back.

TAKING ONE STEP BACK TO TAKE MANY STEPS FORWARD AS A FAMILY

Now, if you have a perfect family—the kind that never argues, never gets their feelings hurt, and where everyone always does the right thing in regards to loving and serving each other—then you can feel free skip ahead to the next chapter. (But before you do, ask your spouse or children if they agree with just how perfect you are!)

But for the other 99.9 percent of us who try hard but often fail at being the parent or grandparent, husband or wife, son or daughter we really want to be—it's time to ask some hard questions.

IT'S TIME TO ASK OURSELVES HARD QUESTIONS

Though the "perfect" family is impossible to come by, some people still put that kind of unrealistic expectation on pastors and their families. However, these committed servants struggle just as much as anyone else when it comes to having

a strong family. Take a good friend who shared a touching story with me recently.

This pastor recounted how he had rushed home from his church one night in order to eat dinner. Few words were spoken at the table, however, as he sat with his wife and their teenage son and daughter. He was lost in thought as he mentally reviewed his day while busy wolfing down his food in order to head off to yet another evening commitment.

"I gotta run," my friend announced, without making eye contact with anyone in the family. "It's Tuesday night and that means I've got to go make my visitation calls." As he got up to leave, he heard his daughter's voice.

"Dad," she said, "can I ask you a question before you go?"

"Sure, honey," he said, turning back to look at her.

"Daddy, next week, can you visit our family?"

You can imagine the heartache that flooded over this father. Here he was, trying to grow a church, going the extra mile by going out at night to visit the sick and shut-ins. He was working hard to do the right thing...but had to face the fact that when it came to his own family, his absence caused his children to feel like orphans.

To my wise friend's credit, he walked back to the table, sat down, and canceled his plans to go out that evening. Instead, beginning with his daughter, he went around the table, asking questions and finding out to his amazement that his son and wife felt the same. They all felt he was never there for them.

"That was the hardest conversation I've ever had with my family or anyone," he told me, "but it turned out to be the absolute best. That night I told them how sorry I was for not being there for them, and I asked what I could do differently—that's when things began to change..."

My friend was fortunate to have a daughter willing to risk hurting or upsetting her father to tell him the truth. (As was she, to have a father with a good enough heart to listen to her concerns.)

GREAT RELATIONSHIPS BEGIN WITH THOSE WILLING TO "UNTIE THE KNOT"

There is an oft-quoted Bible verse that reads, "You will know the truth, and the truth will set you free" (John 8:32 NIV). The Greek word for "to set free" is interesting. It literally means "to untie the knot," and it's the same word that is translated elsewhere, "forgiveness."

Do you get the "picture" that this word carries?

What we're suggesting in this first look at what it takes to have a close-knit home is that, in order to deal with anger and indifference in a home, you need

truth and forgiveness. Anger ties people in knots and indifference puts a double knot on top and cinches it tight. But facing the truth and being willing to ask for forgiveness—and giving it when it's asked of us—"unties the knots" and sets us free to really connect closely with others.

THREE LITTLE WORDS...

Dr. Joe White is the head of six tremendous youth camps near Branson, Missouri. Each summer thousands of teenagers attend these camps. One year Joe gave each camper a survey, and on it was the question:  "What would you most like to hear from your parents?"

The answer the staff received back from several thousand high school students surprised them. In writing the survey, the counselors were certain that what most teenagers would like to hear were the

25

three words, "I love you." But while those are three great words to say to a teenager, early and often, they weren't the words these kids most wanted to hear.

Actually, they wanted to hear two words, not three. "I'm sorry."

Do you know what it takes for an electrical light to turn on? You have to have a closed circuit. If you have an open loop in the circuit—a break in the wiring somewhere—the light never goes on. The same thing is true for a family. The reason so many homes never light up from the inside is that there are open loops. Breaks in the circuit.

Forgiveness helps close loops and lights up homes. So here's a practical, challenging assignment if you're serious about lighting up your home with God's love and your own. Don't wait for your spouse or son or daughter to stop you at the dinner table to tell you that things need to change. Don't wait for your parents or a sibling to show up at your doorstep and say, "I'm sorry. It was my fault."

Put away the pride that says, "It's not my problem" or "That's just the way I am" or "It was their fault" and remember something important.

The stronger person initiates the peace.

The stronger person is the one willing to untie the knots.

And a strong family requires a willingness for people to say when they are wrong, "I'm sorry. What can I do to make things better, or to be a better person?"

Asking people to admit they were wrong and to take responsibility to make things right is rather a hard way to start this book, I know. But I never said that having a strong family was going to be easy. In fact, I'll be the first to admit that it goes against my grain to have to admit when I'm wrong. But I've learned that it doesn't cause me to lose ground in my marriage or with our daughters when I do. *In fact, the opposite is true.* I gain ground as a husband and father, and I become a model for my children when I exhibit the strength it takes to assume personal responsibility for wrong actions by saying, "I'm sorry. How can I make this right?"

A STRONG FAMILY REQUIRES A WILLINGNESS FOR PEOPLE TO SAY WHEN THEY ARE WRONG, "I'M SORRY. WHAT CAN I DO TO MAKE THINGS BETTER, OR TO BE A BETTER PERSON?"

In a later chapter, we'll talk about how to come to grips with someone (like a parent) who never will say they're sorry or admit they're wrong. But we don't have to stay tied up in "knots" ourselves. We can be persons strong enough to forgive and say "we're sorry" to open doors we may have shut.

For now, more than ever, we need to face past hurts and take responsibility.

Carving Out Time for Close Relationships

Thomas Kinkade

"But you just don't understand!" she told me. "It's not going to work. I'm sick of trying. It hasn't gotten any better."

These were the words of a woman who came into my counseling office with her husband. Not that she *wanted* to come into the office, mind you. But her father, who was paying for her divorce attorney, said he wouldn't pay a cent to her lawyer unless she came for counseling first. Which meant I was told I had four sessions to change things between them or she was gone.

Four sessions isn't much time, so I decided to take up a good part of the first session by reading her a story. Now if that sounds to you like wasting good time in the face of a looming deadline or a lack of due diligence on the part of a counselor…well, that's just what she said! But that was *before* she heard the story.

What follows is a story that turned this couple's relationship around. It may not seem as though it has a lot to do with having a strong family when you begin to read it…but look closer. It's actually a beautiful scene, painted by a master artist, that captures the second picture of a strong family we'd like to share with you.

"WHY BOTHER…IT'S NOT GOING TO WORK."

The winter of 1498 was memorable for its bitter cold. The city of Florence, Italy, was blanketed in snow, and Michelangelo Buonarroti's heart was as heavy as the gray clouds that dipped low and blocked out the sun.

The Grand Duke of Florence, Lorenzo de' Medici, had been the young artist's benefactor. It was this great supporter of the arts who had given Michelangelo the numerous slabs of marble he needed to refine his incredible talents. But before Michelangelo was able to create his masterpieces, his source of marble was cut off. The old duke died, and his son, Piero, had no use for a sculptor on the payroll. That went double for wasting good money on marble. So, the artist's great talents were put on the shelf, and Michelangelo sat and waited. That is, until a few days before a great party at the new duke's palace.

In what looked like an incredible answer to his prayers, Michelangelo was summoned before Piero. He'd never been to the palace, even when the Grand Duke had been alive, and he hurried down the streets, past the guards, and in to see Duke Piero.

While he was afraid to believe it, the rumor circu-lated by the servant who came to fetch Michelangelo was that he was being commissioned to carve a great statue! At last!

When Michelangelo arrived at the palace, he was ushered into a large room where not only Duke Piero de' Medici but also a crowd of the duke's friends awaited his arrival. He was indeed told that his  services as a sculptor were needed by his new patron. All he had to do was to go down to the garden, and he'd find all the white marble he needed to make a masterpiece for the duke's party.

Can you guess by now what the duke was actually asking Michelangelo to do? All the white marble in the garden was…snow. Perhaps the greatest sculptor of all time had been brought to the palace to create a snow sculpture for a royal dinner party!

Just imagine for a moment what was going

through Michelangelo's mind as he walked from the room and down to the garden. If it had been me, I'd have been furious. What an embarrass-  ment! What a colossal waste of time—to put all that effort into something that would melt as soon as the sun broke through the clouds!

Michelangelo could have stormed out or at least left the duke's presence with an angry, unwilling heart. Instead, he simply went to work. Hour after hour he gathered snow into a great mound. Then, at last, he began to carve.

Working from the top down (when normally you carve from the base on up), a head appeared, and then shoulders, limbs, torso, and legs. A figure was emerging from the white snow that would be viewed as a joke by Duke Piero and his guests, and then melt away in no time.

Yet still, Michelangelo worked. That's because he had decided in his heart that *even if all he could do was make Florence a more beautiful place for a few hours—he would put all his heart into carving that block of snow.* And then it came time for Piero's party.

The guests arrived. The snow carving finally was unveiled…and instead of laughter came breathless silence. The duke and his guests were staring in awe and amazement at the figure in the snow that seemed able to breathe and walk and even sling a rock at a giant. For that statue made of snow was created by Michelangelo to represent the Bible's David.

The duke was silenced by the tireless efforts of the young artist who had created a masterpiece made out of snow.

Then, amazingly, that statue turned to marble.

IN GOD'S EYES, EVERY SINGLE ACT OF FAITHFULNESS IS NOTED.

Not that hour of course, for it wasn't magic. But in the days that followed, Michelangelo's David was replicated in marble—given him by none other than Duke Piero himself. This priceless work has drawn millions of people to Florence since it was unveiled— all because Michelangelo was willing to carve something of beauty out of snow….

Which—I'm sure you were waiting for this—brings us to the second picture of a strong family and the effect this story had on that young woman in my office.

Nearly every day, people walk into my counseling office feeling as though they're wasting their time carving snow statues. Why bother to put effort into a relationship that's doomed to fail? Why try so hard when all the talking and praying and trying we're doing is just going to melt when things heat up.

Why bother to try—after all, it's just snow.

That's also what it can seem like for the person who tries to do an excellent job for a boss who doesn't appreciate his or her efforts. Or for parents

God always rewards faithfulness

who work so hard to raise kids who never seem to say thanks. Or for the high school student who is  tempted to quit practicing when she's stuck on third string on the basketball team. Or the grown child who spends countless hours taking care of an aging parent who gives zero thanks. *Do our efforts matter?*

Absolutely—because God always rewards faithfulness.

The effort you put into building a strong family, or continuing to work on a struggling marriage, or increasing your faith, or creating something as lasting as you can at work, may seem as though you're carving snow—but in God's eyes, every single act of faithfulness is noted. You're carving marble to Him when you stay faithful even when it's tough.

You can take King David's word on that.

"To the faithful you show yourself faithful," says the shepherd-turned-king in one of his psalms. God hangs out with faithful people—even if all they think they're accomplishing while they're here on earth is carving in the snow.

Week two after hearing this story was when that woman in my office began to hope that her marriage could be better after all. Actions influence feelings, so as she put her whole heart into really trying—as did her husband—she found herself actually relaxing inside. By week three, acts of service had lead to a grudging respect. By week four, that respect had turned to like, and for the next eight weeks (which they paid for), that like turned back into the love they thought they had lost.

That's the second picture of what it takes to have a strong family. The courage, character, hope, and faith to keep trying—even if we think all our efforts are in vain. God rewards such efforts. In this life and in the next.

May each of us be faithful today in doing our

best with the "snow" we're given—for now, more than ever, we need the marble of faithfulness to build strong families.

The Third Picture

MARRIAGES MARKED BY SERVING AND SHARING

I can remember that day as though it were yesterday. The light was streaming in on a beautiful late-spring morning when I opened my eyes. There were only a few weeks left in the semester before final exams…and then the freedom of a summer with no school. I woke up in a good mood and walked down the hallway and into the kitchen, thinking Cindy, my precious wife of only two years at the time, would already be up and have started the coffee.

She was up all right, but she hadn't spent her time making lattes or a big breakfast. Instead, she was getting ready to serve me a picture I've never forgotten in nearly 25 years of marriage.

There in the kitchen, just on the left as I walked in, was the little dinette set we'd bought at an auction. It wasn't worthy of the name antique, even though it did have a semi-50s look with plastic and chrome. What I noticed was actually on the table. There, where I normally sat, was a plate with one of my textbooks on it that I'd been studying for finals.

It was a large book. It was the only thing sitting on the table—and it was dramatically placed on a plate. Even I couldn't miss the fact that this must have been put there purposefully by my bride. So I took the bait.

"What's this?" I smiled. "Is this a new study technique? Digesting your text books for breakfast to make you smarter?"

"No," my wise wife said, "this is how I feel about our relationship. I could have picked any of your textbooks, but this is how I feel about our marriage right now."

Seeing I was not getting her meaning, she went on.

"Right now you're studying really hard, John. That's kind of like how you were when we were dating. You spent lots of time getting to know me. You'd look ahead with me, like you couldn't wait to turn the page and see what was next. You took me seriously. But then we got married and I began to feel like I was one of your books after final exams. It goes up on the shelf, you get busy with other things, and I'm left there with all your other books..."

Needless to say, I got the picture that morning.

In fact, I doubt whether she could have picked a better book to put on my plate. Every time I picked up that textbook between that morning and final exams, I thought again about her words. They haunted me. They made me feel ashamed. Here I was, married

only two years—and in the middle of my doctoral program in marriage and family counseling—and I'd succeeded in making my wife feel like a used, ignored textbook. Some great counselor I was going to be.

Have you ever been there?

On either side of the table?

It was so confusing at the time. We'd had such a great courtship. We hardly had any tense discussions, much less big arguments. It seemed as though we couldn't spend enough time together talking. But that morning, I had to admit deep inside that Cindy was right. I couldn't even get defensive or angry or think of any kind of "cute" comeback. I just said I was sorry, and I asked her to sit down at that nearly worthless table to talk about how we could make our relationship priceless and valuable again.

LET'S GO OUT TO THE MOVIES

I didn't know back then—I didn't have a clue back then—what real intimacy in a marriage looked like. Now, *courtship,* that was different. I could do courtship. That's because I'd seen countless movies that pictured courtship and read the occasional book where guy meets girl—though mostly war novels where the guy marches away. Even today, little has changed when it comes to the movies. From *Sleepless in Seattle* to *The Wedding Planner* or any one of a hundred different romance "flicks" you'll find based on the same premise. Namely, the hard work of the relationship is the courtship.

According to the big screen, it's getting the person to marry you that's the biggest challenge. You assume from watching how happy they are that things will go like a dream from there. But neither by watching movies nor in real life (particularly as I grew up in a single-parent household) did I ever see what happens in a warm, loving marriage. I got married like thousands of people like me—not realizing that the real work of maintaining a strong marriage comes after the wedding.

Somehow, I missed the part in *Sleepless in Seattle* where you see Meg Ryan and Tom Hanks learning how to disagree without damaging each other's sense of self-worth. I must have been out of the room when Harrison Ford in *Sabrina* discovered that helping with the dishes and other chores around the house in the morning had a direct link to how romantic things would be at night.

The pictures we're bombarded with in our culture don't prepare us to deal with the emotions of

Thomas Kinkade

Thomas Kinkade

having to cancel our vacation because all our money has to go into a new furnace, or how to face a crop failure, or how to stay close when you have to walk in the door and tell your spouse, "I lost my job" the same week they lost theirs.

There just aren't many pictures of real love on the big screen that portray a close marriage. But that doesn't mean there aren't pictures that can guide us.

The picture I got that morning from Cindy was a wake-up call that I had to work hard on my marriage if I wanted it to grow and last. M. Scott Peck in his landmark book *The Road Less Traveled* begins with a simple statement of fact: "Life is hard. Once you accept this fact, it becomes easier." Let me paraphrase that observation for those of us who are married.

"Having a strong marriage is hard work. Once you accept that fact, it becomes easier." Once a husband and wife realize they have two full-time jobs—what they do for a living or raising the children or both *and* the full-time effort it takes to keep a marriage strong and growing—things begin to change for the better. But with only four percent of couples having more than one session of premarital counseling, most don't realize this.

Once a husband settles into the fact that he has two full-time jobs, he begins to realize that he isn't coming home just to rest but to relate. Once a wife realizes that blessing and building up her husband is her second full-time job, it changes her inner commitment and caring level. When

THE REAL WORK OF MAINTAINING A STRONG MARRIAGE COMES AFTER THE WEDDING.

both partners "get" this concept that serving and sharing and building a marriage requires the commitment of a full-time job, I've seen them actually become more patient with one another. They start asking questions to clarify a position instead of just blasting each other. They're less critical, and they

Having a strong marriage is hard work

actually start remembering why they love each other.

Put two people working overtime to have a strong marriage in a home—each one committed to  making deposits of love and respect into their relationship as they would money into a small business bank account—and you've got a great place to come home to. Problems and issues and all, a home where each person works hard at serving and sharing is also a tremendous place for children and grandchildren to be as well.

Ask yourself these questions: If your marriage were a business, would it be making a profit? Would you even *be* in business? Do you have a business plan for your marriage, or are you just winging it, thinking success comes without effort. . .just like it does in the movies.

Infatuation takes almost no effort. For example,

you might see someone from across the room—like the first time I saw Cindy—and fall head over heels. But intimacy is earned the old-fashioned way. Twenty-three years after I saw Cindy from across a crowded room, we're still in love. Not just because I still think she's beautiful, but because we've both worked full-time to build a strong marriage and keep our home full of light.

Now, more than ever, a strong marriage takes sensitivity, a servant's heart, measured words, and a willingness to commit to building a loving marriage. And for the Trents and Kinkades, there's one more thing that gives us the strength to get up and do those chores when we'd rather not, to help get the children ready in the morning instead of sitting in the car beeping to hurry everyone up. It's the same thing that deepens your love and passion and commitment for your life-partner the way nothing else can or will.

The power source for staying committed and

caring comes from the Author of love Himself. A couple who truly loves God will find themselves growing closer even when the going gets tough. That's because when you look in the Lord's eyes, He keeps reminding you of words such as faithfulness, patience, service, and sacrifice. When you love the Lord, you keep remembering how much He's forgiven you…and you realize it's about time you forgave your spouse for not being perfect. And when couples pray consistently with each other to the God who knows and loves them, there are dramatically fewer divorces. (That's not just a clinical reality. Just try praying together night after night without getting or staying closer! It's really hard to muster up hate for someone you pray with each night!)

I'M BACK IN THE KITCHEN…

Every once in a while when I walk into the kitchen in our house, I look over at our breakfast nook and see the beautiful oak table and chairs Cindy finished herself. That's when I think about the little table we once had, now long gone, and the morning I was served a textbook for breakfast.

By the way, Cindy only served me a textbook once. That's because a wise, beautiful woman who still loves me helped me immensely that morning by giving me a picture I'll never forget.

And speaking of pictures, you've just seen the third picture of a strong family. A picture where each spouse commits to the hard daily work of serving and sharing—aided immensely by loving God—that can build and maintain a lasting relationship.

For now, more than ever, we need strong marriages.

The Fourth Picture

"BEING THERE"
FOR OUR CHILDREN

o you think that skiing is safer than flying on a commercial aircraft? Or that smoking is less dangerous than being around handguns? Or that nuclear power plants are riskier than cars? Or that more Americans die of homicide than suicide? Or that AIDS is more lethal than kidney disease?

If you're like the average American, you answered most of these questions incorrectly. These were the findings of Dr. Paul Slovic at the University of Oregon, who has spent decades studying how we decide what's risky and what isn't. Objective statistics find that skiing and smoking and cars and suicide and kidney disease are far more lethal than what they're compared to above. What causes this major difference between the real level of risk and the risk level we feel inside?

Namely, people tend to underestimate risk when they think they're in control. For example, the average person feels more in control and safer in their car than when a pilot is flying them somewhere.

Now what does all that talk of risk have to do with having a strong family—and especially being a loving parent? Actually, a lot more than you might think.

TAKE THE RISK TO "BE THERE"
FOR YOUR KIDS

In a landmark study in *Pediatrics*, the journal of the American Academy of Pediatrics, Dr. James Sargent of Dartmouth Medical School found that parents overrated another risk factor. Namely, the risk of really engaging their children—especially as they get older.

"We overrate the rebelliousness of teenagers," said Dr. Sargent.

"That works to our disadvantage…[because] parents underestimate their influence on their children. They have an overly heightened concern about coming down hard on their kids about things like smoking because they think it's going to make them more rebellious. Just the opposite is true."[2]

As we look at our fourth picture of what makes a strong family, we can see another essential for having a home full of light. Namely, it takes loving parents who are willing to "be there" for their children—even if it that means facing their fears of rejection and confronting their children on issues of right and wrong.

Particularly when children are young, there's a saying you hear constantly on advertisements that

moms and dads should take to heart. "You must be present to win."

Being physically present for a child is absolutely critical. We should make every effort to keep our hobbies from keeping us from our kids. And we should use "other care" as little as humanly possible. But even this may not be enough. I've counseled with  hundreds of grown children who grew up feeling as though their mom or dad was never "there" for them—and yet their parents were always at home.

To be there for a child means much more than just sleeping under the same roof. It means that *our name and our eyes and our hearts are there for them*—always. Let me briefly explain what all that means.

Many years ago, there was an amazing grand opening of sorts. It involved the entire nation of Israel and the dedication of their first Temple. Basically, for years

they had housed their precious Ark of the Covenant in a large tent called the Tabernacle. At long last, they had a permanent place for the ark. A wonderful temple King Solomon built would now house the ark and become Israel's central place of worship.

But the ceremony and celebration wasn't the best part of the dedication. The best part came after the great Temple had been dedicated. For that was when Almighty God spoke to Solomon and gave him this promise: "I have heard the prayer and plea you have made before me; I have consecrated this temple, which you have built, by putting my Name there forever. My eyes and my heart will always be there" (1 Kings 9:3 NIV).

Can you imagine the security the nation of Israel felt at that time? They finally had a temple, and they had the Lord's word that He wasn't going anywhere. Forever, His name, eyes, and heart would be there for His people.

Let's apply that to loving parents who need to be

there for their children today. Namely, those same three things that God promised to His people are the commitments we need to make to our children.

Forever—meaning way beyond what is convenient or cultural—our children need to know we have our "name" on them. In olden times,  a craftsman would put his name on something to show he was proud of it, and that it was considered worthy to carry his name. Do your children feel that they are of great value to you? Do they know that of all the children in the world you'd put your name on them?

Then there are the eyes we need to have on our children. We need to look for the best in their lives, not the worst. And always, our heart should be there as well. A heart to listen and love, to put ice on boo-boos when they're toddlers and to pray over broken dreams in their teens.

But having our eyes, name, and hearts "be there" are not the only aspects of the job description of a parent who wants a strong family. There's also the need to be strong enough to face up to our children on issues of right and wrong.

BOMBS IN A CHILD'S BEDROOM

During my high school years, there were times I can remember feeling my mother was violating my rights when she refused to let my twin brother, Jeff, and me lock our door. (Except when we were changing.) In part, she needed access in order to get clean laundry in and dirty clothes out. But even more— she wanted to make sure we weren't hiding or doing anything in our rooms that we shouldn't be doing.

How dare she! But she dared. And she also let us know that she wouldn't let us lock our doors because, "If we weren't changing and weren't doing anything wrong, then why couldn't we open the door?"

At times we ranted and raved…but we never did figure out a good answer to her question, and besides that, she stood fast. And guess what? Even though I was upset with her coming into the room, at times I knew she was right. There were times we were tempted to do or bring things into our room that we shouldn't—but with my mom on watch, there was never a safe haven in our home to do wrong.

I can say with almost 100 percent certainty (that is, unless my brother Jeff, who today is a doctor and was always good at science, created something I never knew about) that we never had or made a bomb in our room.

The reason I share that is because I am amazed at how often a newspaper will note that the police found illegal guns or bomb-making materials in the rooms of murderous teens. When I've heard they've found military grade C-4 or 9mm hollow-point ammunition or homemade explosives in a child's or teenager's room, my first question is "Where in the world were their parents?"

Strong parents in strong families know enough to not let their children lock them out of their lives—

TO BE THERE FOR A CHILD MEANS . . .

THAT OUR NAME AND OUR

EYES AND OUR HEARTS ARE THERE

FOR THEM—ALWAYS.

or things like drugs, immoral materials, or, for a few, even bombs can end up in hormone-driven or angry kids' rooms. It takes effort and courage to face up to our children at times, and a willingness to face their anger or displeasure when we care enough to confront them in love.

So to live out this fourth picture of a strong family, it takes a loving parent who commits to "forever" having their name, eyes, and heart watch over their child. And as part of "being there," we must have the strength to stand up for what's right and wrong.

You must be present to win

The Fifth Picture

AFFIRMING COURAGE IN OUR CHILDREN

ebecca and Abigail Bates lived in a lighthouse on the coast of Massachusetts near the small village of Scituate. Their father kept the light shining at the harbor entrance to guide ships away from the rock-strewn coast.

One day in 1814, their mother and father left the lighthouse in charge of the young girls while they used their rowboat to reach a nearby village. As the girls performed their assigned chores, they saw a ship come around the point. This wasn't just any ship—it was a British frigate, and America was at war with Great Britain. British ships would often try to sneak in using rowboats filled with soldiers to attack villages. In fact, Scituate had already been sacked once, and the British had left ten American ships burning in the harbor.

There were no adults around. Just Rebecca and Abigail. But the village had to be warned. Perhaps the British could be stopped if the sisters found a way to call for help. What happened next saved Scituate and showed incredible bravery.

British rowboats full of soldiers left the frigate and rowed steadily toward shore. But the two girls had done some quick thinking...and praying. They ran into the lighthouse, where Abigail took her father's drum and Rebecca took a fife. They quickly hid themselves in a clump of cedar trees near the shoreline. Just before the soldiers stepped out of their boats, the British heard the beating of a drum and the playing of "Yankee Doodle" on a fife! Thinking the local militia were in hiding and had been called into line to rake the boats with musket fire, the British troops fell over themselves getting back in their rowboats and raced back to the mother ship. The village was saved!

Any parent would be proud if their children had displayed Abigail and Rebecca's kind of ingenuity and courage. Thankfully, few children will have to face the kind of danger these two patriot sisters did, but it is important for our sons and daughters to learn how to show courage under fire, even in life's smaller battles.

AFFIRMING COURAGEOUS CHOICES
CAN LIGHT UP YOUR HOME

As parents, we need to affirm a son who goes and gets a teacher to rescue a friend from a playground bully; or a daughter who keeps working hard to get good grades, even when she is ridiculed by others for being "too smart" or "teacher's pet." We need to affirm the child who shows courage and discipline to come back from a sports injury, or the twins who choose friends that want to do right, not wrong.

APPLAUDING SMALL ACTS OF COURAGE
IN DAILY LIFE

The fifth picture of a strong family is affirming courage in our children, even when their acts of bravery may seem small. Take an act of courage that recently took place at a Youth Basketball game where we live.

A father I know was an All-State athlete when he was young, and now is his son's  coach. Picture a *competitive* person who still is in good enough shape to go out on the court and play. But also picture a father who is wise enough to see a courageous act for what it is and can praise his son for it—even though it cost his team a play-off game.

With under two minutes left in their basketball game and his team up by only one point, there was a scramble for the ball. Ten-year-old Matthew, the coach's son, heard the referee make the call when the ball went out of bounds—"Blue ball!"

Matthew's team had possession! They could run out the clock or run up their lead. But Matthew knew something the referee apparently didn't. He walked over to the referee and said, "I touched the ball last, Ref."

There was a pause as the referee looked intently at him. Then he yelled, "Red ball! Red ball!" and switched possession to the other team.

I realize this was Youth League, not the NBA. But I can also picture many coaches, especially many competitive fathers in the coaching ranks, who would have come *unglued* if their son decided to have an integrity attack in the last two minutes of the game. Many fathers—some I've seen coach my own kids—would have called their son "stupid" for owning up to what Matthew did, not courageous. But not my friend.

"Way to go, Matthew!" he said, and he meant it. The other team went on to score and ended up winning a close game. It was a costly lesson in doing

Courage to do the right thing, which is an important part of a home of light, is cultivated when parents affirm right choices.

what is right, but Matthew's father chose to affirm his son's decision as courageous.

Why is it so important to affirm such acts? Fast-forward 20 years, and I'd want someone with Matthew's courage and integrity to make the hard decisions if he were operating on me, or representing me in negotiations, or leading our country, or pastoring a church, or being the kind of person our daughter marries.

Courage to do the right thing, which is an important part of a home full of light, is cultivated when

63

parents affirm right choices. Even if it's something as simple as writing a poem.

LOOKING AROUND YOU TO PRAISE
SMALL ACTS OF COURAGE

A few days after the World Trade Center fell, Cindy and I witnessed our daughter Laura do something courageous. It began early on the morning of September 11 as our family of four watched in horror as the first tower, and then the second, came crashing down.

Laura was only in fifth grade. She couldn't rush into the Twin Towers the way the heroic New York City firefighters did, or try to help others in the manner of the Port Authority and those brave police officers. Instead, Laura sat down later that day in her room and thought and prayed and cried for all the lives lost. Then she wrote a poem she titled "Now, More Than Ever." We had talked about this theme during the day, but the following words (and spelling and grammar) are all her own:

NOW MORE THAN EVER...

Now more than ever we need to stand strong,

Now more than ever we need to be one,

Now more than ever we need to fight back,

To prove what is right, to prove we are strong

Now more than ever we need to hold on,

To keep our country together

and our flag waving long,

Now more than ever we need to have friends.

Families will struggle but will win in the end,

Now more than ever we need our God,

He'll help us with pain and He'll help us with life.

Let's stand up and help each other

through this struggle of faith

Let us never forget the tears that we've shed

Of those who are lost and those who are dead

Now more than ever we need to stand strong,

To fight all the evil, Lord please keep us strong.

I realize it's the poem of an 11-year-old, not Tennyson. But it took courage for Laura to share her poem at the dinner table that night. It took courage for her to turn it in to her teacher the next day at school and to listen to some of her classmates snicker when her teacher asked her to read it to the class. Whether you're 11 or 111, it takes courage to write down your feelings and lay them before others.

And for that, we praised Laura for her conviction to share what she felt God had put on her heart.

Three days later on Friday night, I saw another example of childlike courage in Kari, our older daughter. After much debate by the local school boards, the high school football games went on as scheduled in Arizona. That meant that Kari, a sophomore cheerleader on the varsity squad, would be cheering on the Eagles.

This was the first football game of the season, and the first game Cindy and I would get to see the

Now more than ever . . .

new cheer squad in action. The year before, Kari, along with five other freshmen and one sophomore, had surprised themselves and everyone by winning the Arizona State Cheerleading competition for small schools! When tryouts were held for the next year's squad, almost 40 girls came out.

A dozen girls made the varsity squad, and as we watched them perform that Friday night after September 11, my heart filled with pride and my eyes misted with tears. I wasn't choked up because of the emotion of the night, but because my heart was touched by the courage of Kari and her cheerleader friends—particularly the last cheerleader selected.

Her name is Brooke, a senior at Kari's school. She may sound like any other high school senior, but Brooke is confined to an electric wheelchair because of cerebral palsy. Brooke had always wanted to be a cheerleader. She has the smile and the enthusiasm to match any of the girls at school. But you can only dream of being a cheerleader if you can't walk, much less do the jumps and stunts. That is, unless the entire cheer squad and their coaches, Mrs. Lester and Miss Dalia, vote you onto the team. It was a dream come true for this inspirational young lady and a tremendous blessing for each girl and all the fans that night.

> HONORING
> COURAGEOUS
> CHILDREN LIGHTS
> UP THEIR LIVES
> AND OUR HOMES.

Picture two rows of cheerleaders in their sharp white outfits laced with red and blue, their school colors. Kari stood next to Brooke in the front row, and you could tell she was proud to be next to her friend.

When the girls turned to face the field with their hands on hips during the game, Brooke moved the toggle on her motorized wheelchair to face the field with them. When they turned back toward the crowd, Brooke turned with them as well. When they did a chant or cheer, Brooke was right there with them. With her eyes and voice and heart, she was every bit a member of the squad.

I know there was a football game going on that night, but my eyes were more frequently drawn to the sidelines where the cheerleaders performed. I was staggered by the courage Brooke showed in struggling to do each cheer the best she could. I was touched by the way Kari would pick up her pom-poms when Brooke dropped them or make sure Brooke got a drink of water during timeouts. (It's still *hot* in Phoenix on September evenings.) And I was so proud of each and every girl on the cheer squad— Nicole and Kellee and Laura and Lauren and Briana and Becca and Kourtney and Ashley and Sarah and Alexandra and Corrie—who loved Brooke as much as Kari. They, too, came over to encourage Brooke, get her drinks, and tell her she was doing a great job.

To put things in perspective, I attended the Rose Bowl in 1998 when my team, Arizona State, lost to Ohio State in the last 48 seconds of the game. I wasn't moved to tears then. I didn't even remember crying when I was a high school football player and we lost the city championship on a cold November night. But watching Kari and Brooke and the rest of the squad that evening, I kept choking up. I saw courage in ordinary kids doing something extraordinary—which is what our country will need in the stressful days ahead.

WHOM IN YOUR COMMUNITY CAN YOU AFFIRM?

Sure, these little stories of courage didn't win Congressional medals for Matthew, Laura, or Kari, and they aren't as dramatic as beating a drum and playing the fife to scare away British soldiers. But it took courage for Matthew to tell the truth, for Laura to write a heartfelt poem, and for Kari and a team of cheerleaders to reach out and see a classmate for

what she could do, not for what she couldn't.

So the next time your children make a courageous choice, pin a medal on them by pointing their actions out to them and to others, if it's appropriate. Reinforce their virtue, values, resolve, faith, and character.

Honoring courageous children lights up their lives and our homes.

For now, more than ever, our country needs courageous kids who come from strong families.

The Sixth Picture

RECONCILING RELATIONSHIPS

I'm a veteran of exactly one marathon. Running 26.2 miles last year in San Diego was a major achievement for me. The colorful medal I received for finishing the race hangs proudly on the edge of a file cabinet next to my desk. But don't ask me what my finish time was, although I can give you a hint: I came in just *behind* the lady pushing the jogging stroller. Put another way, the men's winner barely nipped me, crossing the finish line a mere two-and-a-half *hours* ahead of my time.

I found out firsthand that with each mile, a marathon becomes more challenging. As the distance increases, so do the extra sweatshirts and fanny packs tossed by runners to the side of the road. Extra ounces can feel like extra pounds by the 20-mile mark.

But what if you had to run that kind of endurance race wearing five-pound ankle weights? That wouldn't be a handicap in a marathon, that would be punishment. With ankle weights, it wouldn't take long before each mile—each step—would become agony. Finishing such a long race would be impossible for all but a few.

"But no one runs marathons with ankle weights!" you might say. I disagree. In fact, I see people arrive every week in my counseling office wearing heavy ankle weights. Some are carrying five, ten, even 20 pounds of emotional weight. It doesn't stop them from walking, but it certainly holds them back from "running a good race," as the apostle Paul calls it (Galatians 5:7 NIV). What's more, those ankle weights are the very things that prevent many people from reaching the goal of having a strong family.

These emotional leg weights, for the most part, are past hurts strapped on tightly by an unwillingness to reconcile relationships. For example, perhaps you left your parents' home in anger as a teenager, but you never closed the loop or made things right with Mom or Dad. That's a ten-pound weight you carry to every family event you do go to, especially during the long holiday season.

Another example would be having a long term relationship break apart and still, years later, be carrying around hatred for the other person. (Not "intense dislike," but acid-dipped hatred.) Hating an ex-spouse can easily be a 20-pound weight—one

that *we* carry, not them—even if they were the ones who walked away from the marriage or hurt the children. Then there are those who suffer a financial setback or are cheated by another person (or both) and make

a decision to despise the one who hurt them. That degree of daily anger can drag down one's ability to enjoy life or build solid relationships.

Using a different metaphor, the apostle John pictures the problem of hating others as causing us to lose direction, focus, and purpose. "The one who says he is in the Light and yet hates his brother is in the darkness until now. . . . But the one who hates his brother is in the darkness and walks in the darkness, and does not know where he is going because the darkness has blinded his eyes" (1 John 2:9,11).

If we're serious about having strong families, we must be free to move forward in life. In chapter 2 we

saw how important it is to face up to and move on from past mistakes in our family. However, for many people, it's the emotional weights with others, not just their immediate family, that cause them to stumble and rob them of the light and energy they need to build a strong family. Thankfully, there's a "new" word that can help us.

SOMETHING "NEW" TO HELP MOVE YOUR LIFE FORWARD

"Learning to Forgive Can Benefit the Forgiver" ran a bold headline from an article in *USA Today* (August 28, 2001). In a study of 259 adults reported by Stanford University psychologist Dr. Carl Thoresen at an annual meeting of the American Psychological Association, those who learned to forgive others saw "stress, anger and psychosomatic symptoms—headaches, stomach upsets, etc.—go way down, significantly lower than for the control group." Likewise, Case Western psychologist Julie Exline concurred, discovering that just writing about a

painful incident (for example, writing a letter but never sending it) can "dispel bad feelings."

Isn't it amazing how the "mounting evidence" confirms what the Bible has told us all along: We gain life, freedom, and direction when we forgive, and we gain stronger families and homes of far brighter light as well.

Dr. Thoresen's study also noted: "A forgiving nature may also improve intimate relationships. Compared with people reluctant to forgive, the forgivers saw romantic partners in a more positive light and reported a more loving relationship."

Translation: Strong marriages and families are inhabited by people who don't explain away or minimize wrong, but who get rid of the ankle weights of hate or bitterness as best they can and as quickly as possible.

It's worth recalling that the Greek word for "forgiveness" means to "untie the knot." That's why I used the image of ankle weights laced up tight to describe

a person who refuses to forgive or deal with past relationships. The more weighed down we are, the less we're free to run alongside each other in this thing called life.

I saw that in my relationship with my father.

LEAVING BEHIND MY ANKLE WEIGHTS

For years I hated him. I absolutely hated my father. He left my mother and us three boys when  I was only two months old. I never met the man until my teen years, even though we all lived in the Phoenix area. Even then, he did little to build a relationship with us, and he never once brought up the subject of why he left Mom, nor did he ever say he was sorry.

Then I became a Christian while I was in high school. I'd like to say that on that very night I unshackled my ankle weights of hate for my father, but that wasn't true. Instead of hating him, I just "intensely

Learing to forgive

disliked" him. It took me *years*—until I was almost through college—before I finally faced the fact that I was the one weighed down by my anger, not him. I was the one losing sleep and quality of life as each mile of life passed by, not him.

I purposely called Dad and asked him to meet me at a nearby Red Lobster in Phoenix. When the main course arrived, I got to the main reason I invited him out to dinner. I wanted to ask his forgiveness for being so angry with him all those years.

I didn't ask Dad to explain away his behavior in leaving. I didn't demand that he explain why he still chose to stay out of his sons' lives—and the lives of his grandchildren. I didn't ask for an apology, nor

> WITH GOD'S HELP, WE CAN RELEASE OUR GRIP ON THE PICTURES THAT HAVE STAYED WITH US FOR SO LONG, EVEN THE PAINFUL ONES.

did I expect to receive one, which is good, because he didn't speak any words of regret.

I'm not sure what happened in my father's heart that night when we walked away from the table, but I know what happened in mine. Whoever cleared away our table also found the pair of ankle weights I left behind.

After that Red Lobster dinner, I began to look at my father in a different way. Remember how the apostle John says you walk out of darkness when you forgive but can't see because of the darkness when you don't? Once I forgave my father, I began to actually notice how lonely he was. While he wouldn't talk about his background, I learned later from my Uncle Max how much my father had suffered both as a child and as a soldier fighting in the Pacific during World War II. Without making excuses for what he did or didn't do, I finally could see something of the struggle he'd had. I was able to feel compassion for him.

I wish there were a storybook ending to this story.

Unfortunately, my father died without even knowing the name of my youngest daughter. But on his last day on earth, I was there for him at the hospice on the corner of Tatum and Paradise Village Parkway. I held his hand for hours, prayed for him, and was able to love him because I'd forgiven him—and most of all because I'd been forgiven by a loving God.

With God's help, we can release our grip on the pictures that have stayed with us for so long, even the painful, hurtful ones. We can forgive and be forgiven, replacing the bad memories of the past with images of love and hope and beauty.

Which brings me to the question I'm sure you saw coming at the start of this chapter. Is there a relationship you need to reconcile?

Is there a relationship with a spouse, a former business partner, or even with God that needs to be dealt with?

Are there ankle weights you need to take off—perhaps today?

For now, more than ever, we need to reconcile relationships if our home is to be a place lit up by God's love.

The Seventh Picture

VALUING AND LISTENING TO OUR SENIORS

*I*t's another enduring memory from my childhood. I'm perched up in "my tree" in our front yard, high atop one of three grapefruit trees—one for each boy in the family. My older brother, Joe, had his own tree that was strictly off-limits to anyone else. His tree was located on the east side of the yard, nearest the lamppost. Jeff, my twin brother, had "dibs" on the tree closest to the carport on the west side of the yard. That left "my tree," which was smack dab in the middle of the yard.

As I peek through the branches and look toward the house, I can see inside the bay window. There's my grandfather, sitting in his favorite chair at our old kitchen table. I think I'm hidden, but his sharp gray eyes see me looking at him. He smiles and lifts up his coffee cup in salute with those big, rough carpenter's hands of his.

I wish now that I'd taken that smile as an invitation. I wish I would have climbed out of my tree and perched myself next to that tall Texan that day—the grandfather I never really got to know. But there were so many important things to do when I was seven years old. I had backyard forts to defend and front yard trees to climb.

I'm afraid I'm not alone in having missed opportunities to hear priceless stories about family history, or to gain wisdom from the trials an elder family member faced, or to just sit and let them know how much I love them by listening at length, without looking at my watch.

Too many members of the Baby Boom generation—and now their grown-up children—are letting parents and grandparents and aunts and uncles slip into eternity without ever once having those long

HE SMILES AND LIFTS UP HIS COFFEE IN SALUTE WITH THOSE BIG, ROUGH CARPENTER'S HANDS OF HIS.

talks. Often it's because we're too busy climbing the corporate ladder or tackling another home improvement project—and I can relate.

I know how time-starved we all are, and I also know that making time for long talks with older family members is asking a great deal. But take it from me, someone who is in his late 40s but already has buried his parents, grandparents, and all but one

uncle and aunt: There's an even greater sense of loss when they're no longer around to talk to.

If you're serious about having strong families and homes full of light and are still blessed with living next of kin, there's no better time than now to set aside some hours in your busy schedule for long talks with your seniors. That's something my friend Darryl did recently, and that decision to reach out to a close relative is still impacting both their lives.

MARCHING BACK THROUGH TIME

A tremendously popular HBO program that debuted during 2001 was *Band of Brothers*, based on a book by Stephen Ambrose. Ambrose's story and the HBO series by the same name follow a company of airborne rangers (Charlie Company, 501st Airborne) from the time they jumped into Normandy on D day until the end of the war outside Berlin.

On a flight from Michigan to Phoenix, I sat next to my good friend, Darryl, who told me about a special trip he'd just made to see his favorite uncle,

who happened to be in poor health. Darryl's Uncle Jim had fought with his own "band of brothers" as a member of the 527th Airborne from D day to VE (Victory in Europe) day.

Darryl shared that he'd picked up a car at the airport and driven a couple hours to his uncle's home. Following a warm greeting, the first thing Uncle Jim did was bring out his wedding pictures. Standing in those faded photographs was a four-year-old boy—Darryl! The photos were taken during the early days of World War II when Darryl was the ring bearer in his uncle's wedding. One picture showed the smiling four-year-old dressed in a military uniform tailored just for him, marching down the aisle of the church. Then, shortly after Uncle Jim said, "I do," he marched off to the European theater.

Uncle Jim was a card-carrying member of "The Greatest Generation," a war hero who parachuted into Holland, participated in the liberation of France, backtracked to save American forces trapped in the

Thomas
Kinkade

Battle of the Bulge, fought his way across the Rhine, and lived to make it to Berlin. That day he talked to Darryl about everything from the wedding photos  to family history questions. How he first met his wife. What he did before the war and immediately afterward. And then, as the conversation warmed, Darryl asked his uncle what it was like being a paratrooper during one of the great military campaigns of the twentieth century.

Uncle Jim was quiet for a long moment. Finally, he breathed deeply, stood up and walked to a back room. He returned several minutes later with an old, creased shoebox. Slowly, he took off the lid, revealing a jumble of decorations for valor from France and Belgium, a Silver Star, and his Purple Heart. Each ribbon had a story. Each story brought back a flood of memories. And each memory brought to the surface long-suppressed feelings his uncle had pushed to the back of his mind.

Tears flowed that afternoon—both from Uncle Jim and from Darryl. Tears as Uncle Jim shared about the horrible sight of being the first one to reach a glider full of dead men the day after D day. Of gunmetal being so cold at Bastone that it would rip the skin off your hands. Of watching your best friend take a sniper's bullet in the neck as he stood only three feet from you—and having him die in your arms *three weeks* before the war was over.

Afternoon turned to evening, and they made sandwiches and soup. All that time the stories continued. Finally, it was time for Darryl to drive the two hours back to where he'd spend the night and then hook up with me for the flight home to Phoenix.

But Darryl's uncle wanted to share two last things with him…his box and his thanks.

"It's for you," said Uncle Jim, as he handed over his box. "I'm real sick, Darryl, you know that. And I'd

Thank you for asking. . .

like you to have these. I think they'd mean something to you."

Darryl protested. Such priceless pictures of heroism and sacrifice should go to his own children, not a nephew. But Uncle Jim insisted, forcing the old shoe box under his arm.

"You're the only one who's ever asked," Uncle Jim said.

"What do you mean?"

"None of my children have ever sat down with me like this," he replied. "Not one of the three ever asked about what happened to me before the war, or during the war, like you. Thank you for asking."

GO SIT AT THE KITCHEN TABLE IF YOU CAN

I'm back, sitting in my tree. . .peeking through the leaves at my grandfather sitting at the kitchen table. Forty-two years later, I wish I'd been wise enough to go inside and have a long talk with him. I can actually remember feeling a pang of guilt back then, but that impulse was interrupted when I had to

repel invaders (my two brothers) from trying to climb my tree.

I thought there would always be time to sit at the kitchen table and talk with Grandfather. You know, someday when the weather wasn't so nice. Then came St. Patrick's Day, just a few weeks later. That day etched another memory, but one much more sorrowful. That was the day my grandfather passed away suddenly inside the house while we kids were playing outside.

In Hebrews 3:7-8 there's a strong admonition not to wait when it comes to seeking out God. "Today, if you hear his voice, do not harden your hearts" (NIV). That's because we may only have today to respond.

By application, I feel a similar focus on "today" is crucial in our personal relationships—and especially with our seniors. Today, if you're serious about having a strong family, don't overlook the seniors in your life. Parents and aunts and uncles may want to share their hearts with *you* as much as you want to hear from them. You can also seek out older friends in your neighborhood or church because they have much to share as well—not just stories, but wisdom and love and insight into others. People in past generations occupied their minds less with technology and more with people. You may be surprised at the wonderful insights they can't wait to share.

But that means climbing down from your perch in the tree and sitting at the kitchen table. My grandfather's death taught me a valuable lesson—one that helped me during my teen years. I made a point then to sit down with my grandmother and have a number of "long talks." I learned so much about the Thomasons and Harts and Trimbles and other assorted relatives in Indiana, and what it was like for her to grow up on a farm, to get married at 16, and to lose everything when Kansas turned into a dustbowl.

I remembered that lesson of having long talks even in the midst of raising young children and

building a career—long talks with Cindy and long talks with my mother. And now that my mother has passed away, I've *never* regretted one moment sitting at her kitchen table.

Isn't it time you sat down with a close family member you love? It may be later than you think, for now, more than ever, we need to have long talks with our seniors.

The Eighth Picture

REMEMBERING TO SMILE

t was December 24, 1944. Christmas that year was a tough time for our country, especially for one young Marine sitting stiffly in an overcrowded train. This was day two of four days and four nights that Corporal Edward Andrusko would spend traveling by train from San Diego to New York. Each passenger car was packed with sailors, soldiers, and Marines trying to get home for Christmas.

Already they had traveled through bleak deserts, a blizzard in Denver, and what seemed like endless frozen prairies and farmland. The whole trip inched by under unrelenting gray clouds, but time didn't seem to matter. Nothing seemed to matter. Recovering from his third wound received in battle and a painful case of malaria, Corporal Andrusko

would arrive home in New York the day *after* Christmas. Even that seemed fitting.

"*I would miss Christmas at home by a day,*" he wrote afterward. "*My parents had split up, and I had no home to go to. My girlfriend of four years sent me a Dear John letter, saying she had waited too long for me to return and found someone else. And worst of all, when I was well enough for duty, I could be sent overseas to battle again.*"[3]

Darkness had fallen, and the train had stopped at a small, dimly lit railroad station about two hours outside Chicago. Large snowdrifts blocked any view from the train. In that cold, dark tunnel of a station, peace and light and love—even thoughts of a loving God—seemed nonexistent.

Earlier in the evening, Andrusko had spoken with a fellow Marine nicknamed "Ski" who was returning home minus his right arm. *"Ski and I agreed that we both became near atheists and cynics after three years of war,"*[4] he remembers. But for one Marine at least, all that would change with a smile.

"IT CAME UPON A MIDNIGHT CLEAR . . ."

Few men were awake as they sat at the station, but Andrusko's war wound and the malaria his body fought made sleep a challenge—particularly having to sleep sitting up the entire trip. But at that dark moment in his young life, the door at the other end of the train car opened.

From Andrusko's seat far in the back, he could barely see a small boy and an elderly lady enter the car. He lost sight of them altogether as they walked slowly down the isle. Apparently they were looking for a seat. Andrusko closed his eyes and tried to go back to sleep, but a noise near him caused him to open his eyes. Standing right in front of him was the young boy and the lady.

"Welcome home and Merry Christmas, Marine." The young boy smiled as he extended his little hand.

"My grandmother and I would like to give you a gift and thank you for serving our country." The little boy shook the wounded  Marine's hand and handed him a crumpled one dollar bill. His grandmother put her arm around him and said, "God bless you." And then they both smiled and said, "Merry Christmas, and goodbye."

Andrusko tried to grab his sea bag from under the seat to try to find a candy bar or some kind of gift he could give them, but when he looked up, they were gone—so quickly that he wondered if what just happened was real or a dream. Later, he asked

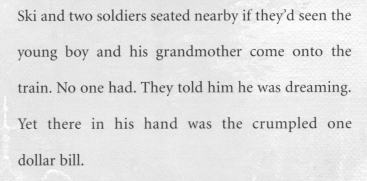

Ski and two soldiers seated nearby if they'd seen the young boy and his grandmother come onto the train. No one had. They told him he was dreaming. Yet there in his hand was the crumpled one dollar bill.

With that smile and small gift, "*I contentedly fell asleep with my precious gift tucked safely in my pocket,*" he recounted, "*and a pleasant feeling in my heart, the nicest feeling I had had in a very long time.*"[5]

Corporal Andrusko credits that night with changing his bitter feelings after the war. But in his mind, it took another child, many years later, to explain to him why that was true.

More than 50 years passed, and the Marine on the train was now as old as the grandmother he'd met that night. It was Christmastime again, and Corporal Andrusko was surrounded by his family gathered for a Christmas celebration, not a train full of weary soldiers. During a lull in the activity, he recounted to everyone the story of the little boy on the train. It was the reminiscing of a soldier grown

old. As he finished, Andrusko asked a question, really to no one in particular: "Who was that little boy on the train, and why did he and his grandmother choose me? Why me?"

A young niece was visiting, and she had listened to her uncle's wartime story and his unanswered questions. "I know," she said quietly.

Everyone stopped to look at her.

The old Marine said, "You know what?"

"I know who the little boy on the train was, and why he picked you." She paused, very deliberately, and then said,

"The little boy was God, and he chose you because you were very, very sad and disappointed with everyone and everything. He wanted to make you happy again and welcome you home—and he did."[6]

Out of the mouth of another child came words of healing and light—and a smile. You can argue the point theologically, but you'll never convince an old Marine and a young child that God didn't show up in that train, wrapped in the warm smile of a young boy.

And God's love still shows up today on the smiling faces of children and adults.

A SMILE CAN LIGHT UP THE DARKNESS

Smiles and laughter didn't end on a blood-soaked Pacific island for a wounded Marine, nor did they die in the burial ground the World Trade Center became on September 11. Certainly then our hearts were robbed of mirth and eyes filled with tears. But in words of the psalmist, "Weeping may last for the night, but a shout of joy comes in the morning" (Psalm 30:5). That's because we are people with hope. Again the psalmist encourages us with the words, "Light arises in the darkness for the upright" (Psalm 112:4).

Even for those who are hurting, laughter can help lift their load. Put in biblical terms, "Bright eyes

gladden the heart; good news puts fat on the bones," says Proverbs 15:30. As difficult a time as our nation faces today, one of the great American character traits we possess is our faith in God that gives us the ability to smile, to joke, and even to laugh at ourselves in difficult times.

Laughter and smiles are signs of strength of character, not of weakness. Returning again to the psalmist, we read: "Then our mouth was filled with laughter and our tongue with joyful shouting; then they said among the nations, 'The LORD has done great things for them'" (Psalm 126:2). Our joy can be a witness to the world of our hope that lies within.

SMILES ARE GOOD MEDICINE FOR THE HEART

There is an old Norwegian proverb that says, "He who laughs, *lasts.*" Numerous clinical studies show that laughter increases blood flow, lowers blood pressure, increases endorphin levels, and even decreases occurrences of second heart attacks. In short, medical science keeps proving what the Bible noted hundreds of years ago. "A joyful heart is good medicine" (Proverbs 17:22).

Certainly, there are things in life that can rob us of our smile—if we let them. For example, I remember when my mother first began to struggle with rheumatoid arthritis. Over the course of several years, I watched her go from hiking desert hills to struggling to get down the hall with a cane. The arthritis forced her to retire from a job she loved and lose the ability to open jars or pick up grandchildren. But she never lost her smile. As she lay dying in a hospice near our home, one of her nurses told me, "John, I know you're mother's hurting, but she glows whenever I come in."

Tragedy and trial are not laughing matters. But it's still healthy to laugh...and to smile...even at strangers. For you never know whose day you'll make.

ONE LAST LOOK AT A GREAT CROWD
FULL OF SMILES

On the night when Corporal Andrusko met the little boy and his grandmother, he tells how the train pulled into Chicago's main train station around midnight. As he looked out the train window, hundreds of people of all ages and all races serenaded the soldiers with Christmas carols and passed out trays of food and drinks to them.

What a wonderful picture of the difference Christmas Day can make in the life of a wounded Marine...and in the life of a nation. Even in the midst of a war, the birth of the Christ child brings joy in the darkness—the Light of the world.

> LAUGHTER AND SMILES ARE A SIGN OF STRENGTH OF CHARACTER, NOT OF WEAKNESS.

The Ninth Picture

Opening Our Eyes
to a Strong Faith

Thomas Kinkade

Try on this plot for a modern-day thriller.

A nation of zealots decides to launch a clandestine war against its much larger neighbor. Knowing they'll be defeated in direct battle with their enemy, they instead plan a series of ambushes that will kill as many people as possible. Even though they can't win in open warfare, these special ops killings will give them victory after victory until the larger nation finally agrees to their demands.

Confident of their strategy, these killers pick several "high value" targets, carefully set their first big ambush, and then wait for the jaws of death to snap shut on those they hate. But when the day of death arrives, no one walks into the prearranged killing zone. No one!

The first time their deadly planning doesn't pay off, they attribute it to blind luck on behalf of their enemy. Patiently, methodically, another target is set. Another day of destruction is planned for those they hate, but the same thing happens—not a single target comes within range!

Now they know their secret operation has been compromised. They have no idea if the CIA, FBI, or NSA has hacked into their operational plans, but they're certain there's a problem. Most likely, it involves a traitorous mole.

They scour their headquarters, where someone

finally finds a long-range listening device inside the commander in chief's personal office. No wonder their plans have been thwarted! Using their own intelligence, they track the device back to its source—a safe house where a known spy master is living. This time, instead of sending killer squads, the furious leader orders hundreds of soldiers to surround the source of the leak in the middle of the night. They will eradicate him and his men in the morning, and then start planning their killing missions all over again.

Just minutes before they launch their attack at dawn, a lowly aide at the spy headquarters walks outside—and he sees the masses of deadly forces silently waiting. He runs back inside crying, "We're surrounded! We're all going to be killed!"

"Calm down," announces the spy master, seemingly unruffled in the face of certain death. "We'll be fine. You just need to slip these on." In his hands are super high-tech laser-vision lenses attached to a headband. "Just look out the window," he says,

handing over the special lenses.

Amazingly, with these goggles on, the aide can see what the terrorists can't. Namely, forming up behind them—invisible to those without the special lenses—are "black ops" helicopters bristling with armed soldiers. With the laser-vision lenses he can see stealth fighters making their final turns, lining up their bomb and strafing runs.

The terrorists are about to go from dangerous to deceased, and the aide goes from fear to faith—because his eyes were opened to a source of help and strength hidden from his sight.

OPEN THE EYES OF OUR HEART, LORD

A possible script from Stephen Spielberg? Not exactly. Try a modern-day version of a story right out of the Bible! The story I'm referring to took place at a time of war for the nation of Israel, and it does indeed hold great parallels and important truths for today.

The Bible shares in 2 Kings 6 how the king of Aram decided to set traps for the soldiers of Israel by sending men to camp out on known roads so that they could ambush and kill them. But time and again, the king's plans were thwarted.

The king of Aram was furious, and he finally found out that the "spy" was none other than the prophet, Elisha, who was relaying information to the king of Israel and averting tragedy for Israel's soldiers.

Just as in the story above, the king of Aram was so furious (discovering you've been spied upon can do that to you) that he sent a host of troops to surround and kill Elisha. Sure enough, a servant of the great prophet went out early one morning and saw their imminent peril. That's when the very first "night vision" goggles were handed out by Elisha to his fearful servant. Not literal goggles, but "eyes of faith."

In that dark hour, with fear gripping his heart, Elisha prays for his servant: *"Do not fear, for those who are with us are more than those who are with them"* (2 Kings 6:16). That's something neither the aide in the imaginary story above nor Elisha's servant could see—until their eyes were opened.

Elisha continues his prayer for his fearful friend, asking Almighty God, *" 'O LORD, I pray, open his eyes that he may see.'* And the LORD opened the servant's eyes and he saw; and behold, the mountain was full of horses and chariots of fire all around Elisha"* (2 Kings 6:17).

The enemy of God's people wasn't victorious that day, nor will they be in our day. Particularly if we learn how to have "eyes of faith" in fearful times.

THE NEED FOR STRONG MENTORS, LEADERS, AND COMMUNITIES OF FAITH

In these days full of anthrax scares and terrorist threats, it's easy to feel that we're surrounded by evil and darkness. Yet it is faith in spite of fear that opens our eyes to see beyond the darkness to the light beyond.

The writer of the book of Hebrews says this about faith: "Faith is the assurance of things hoped for, the conviction of things not seen" (Hebrews 11:1). Great faith in our day means living out a bold faith as well. It means being sure of our hope in a cause that's right before the victory over terror is finished. It means being certain that God cares for us, even when we shake our heads at another act of terror on our shores. It means being confident in the fact that a positive outcome *not* seen is still an outcome that's sure.

GREAT FAITH IN OUR DAY MEANS LIVING OUT A BOLD FAITH AS WELL.

You'll notice as well that the servant of Elisha did at least one thing right in his fear—he ran to a person of strong faith. I submit that those of us who want to build strong families need to draw strength and courage from mentors and leaders who are people of great faith. Where do you find such people, who can be godly examples to you and your children? A great place to begin is your local church.

Whatever city or town you're in, take a look around at those whose lives you have seen changed by going to church—and then follow them Sunday morning or Saturday night.

Just follow a changed life, and you'll be following someone like Elisha's servant, who had his eyes opened. A person who may have been fearful and surrounded by the worst-case scenario, but someone who then found strength in a loving God.

For now, more than ever, we need to follow and become people of strong faith.

The Tenth Picture

BECOMING PEOPLE OF PRAYER

*I*n the *Los Angeles Times* magazine, writer Vince Rause and neuroscientist Andrew Newberg collaborated on an amazing article. It was titled, "Why God Won't Go Away," and it came to the "scientific" conclusion of something our whole country seems to remember in times of great trial. Namely, there is strong evidence that humans are "hardwired" to believe in God.

The natural need to turn to God in prayer has made a dramatic and public comeback since September 11. Just a sampling of headlines in the aftermath of that dark day read:

- "School, Local Govt's Turn to Prayer"
- "We're Letting God Back In"
- "ACLU Take Note: People Are Praying"

But it's not just in the headlines, but in the hearts of Americans that prayer is making a comeback—and it should.

Prayer is like opening a window in a room that's unbearably hot. Prayer brings in the fresh air of hope and comfort. Prayer gives us courage, even as it provides an avenue for our hurt and pain to escape.

Prayer also gives us access to a loving God, even if we've been years in the asking. Just ask my Uncle Max.

A LONG-LOST RELATIVE COMES HOME...

After graduating from high school, money was tight in our single-parent home, and so I stayed home for the first two years of college and saved a bundle on out-of-state tuition and room and board.

I received a big break my junior year when I won a scholarship to attend Texas Christian University—

known by many as TCU and home of the "Horned Frogs"—in Fort Worth, Texas. In my first semester, I received an assignment to write a paper in one class, but I was advised to do my research at the Southern Methodist University library in nearby Dallas. Sure, SMU was a big rival of TCU, but I was told that their library had voluminous amounts of material relating to my subject.

I walked into the SMU library lobby for the first time. To the right side of the circulation desk I noticed a glass-walled office. Upon closer inspection, I read a sign on the door announcing, "Robert M. Trent, Head Librarian."

Another Trent! Still, I knew the name "Trent" was common enough, so the chance of this Mr. Trent being blood kin was rather remote.

But never the shy type, I nonetheless decided to do something smart-alecky. I walked through the wide-open door and announced to the distinguished gentleman sitting at his desk, "Hi, Uncle Robert! I'm your long-lost nephew, John Trent, from Arizona."

I was just kidding, of course, thinking he'd laugh or explain that he didn't have any lost nephews.

Instead he looked at me intensely and asked, "Are you Joe Trent's boy?" My mouth fell open. I had no idea that I had an "Uncle Robert" in Texas. As we compared notes, I learned that he was my *great-uncle*—my father's uncle—but everyone called him by his middle name, Max.

Uncle Max graciously invited me to his home for dinner that night, where I met the love of his life for 45 years, Aunt Sally. She was a diminutive woman with piercing eyes and a wonderful sense of humor. They had never had any children, just each other, but they took a liking to me. I was soon adopted as a regular dinner guest.

One morning, Aunt Sally walked out to the drive-way to pick up the hefty *Dallas Morning News* Sunday edition. At the same time, a tow truck driver—having overshot the address he was looking for—

slammed on his brakes and began hurriedly backing up into the Trent driveway to turn around.

As Aunt Sally bent over to pick up her Sunday paper, she was blissfully unaware that a double-wheeled wrecker was about to back over her.

PRAYER IS LIKE OPENING UP A WINDOW IN A ROOM THAT IS UNBEARABLY HOT. PRAYER BRINGS IN THE FRESH AIR OF HOPE AND COMFORT.

I received a panicked call that morning from Uncle Max, describing the accident and asking whether I could meet him at Baylor Hospital. I raced down the Dallas/Fort Worth Turnpike and arrived at the hospital, where a despondent Uncle Max fell into my arms and informed me that Aunt Sally—on top of her massive injuries—had just suffered a heart attack.

We were told her life was hanging by a thread. As for Uncle Max, his life was also crumbling all around him. There wasn't anything I could do but hug and weep with him.

Up until now, Uncle Max had steadfastly refused to talk about religion. He loved having me over for dinner on Sunday nights, but he made it clear that he didn't want me talking about my faith or my work with Young Life, a Christian campus group. He wasn't interested in anything that smacked of faith. He was a Columbia graduate who held a Ph.D. in library science and had married another Columbia University Ph.D. in library science. He and Aunt Sally had their books and their knowledge, and that's all they needed.

Until that Sunday, when their secure world fell apart.

I asked Uncle Max whether he would mind if I prayed for Aunt Sally. "Please do," he replied. "Please pray for her...and for me."

We found a quiet corner of the waiting room just outside the critical care ward where we prayed for his

wife. I prayed that she would make it through surgery. I prayed that her heart would mend and become strong. I prayed for the doctors and nurses practicing their skills. I prayed for courage, healing, and hope for Uncle Max.

We waited two long days and even longer nights for an answer to that prayer. With each update from a doctor or nurse, however, we were given more to pray about in our little corner, not less. And then in Baylor Hospital, there came a resurrection day of sorts on the third day of waiting. Aunt Sally's primary physician unexpectedly came into the waiting room and asked for Uncle Max.

The news was nothing short of miraculous.

The doctor said that Aunt Sally was now responding in a way that shocked him. He felt he could confidently say that she would not only pull through the heart surgery, but that she would be out of the hospital, predicting that she'd be home within a month. (Turns out, she would beat that

prognostication by a full week.)

When Uncle Max and I received that wonderful news, we hugged and cried, and then I prayed one more time with him. I  thanked the Lord for what we both felt He had done through the surgeon's hands. And then Uncle Max asked me a question that would lead to a changed life for him. He asked, "Would you tell me more about this God we've been praying to?"

Would I? Of course I would! Yet it wasn't my words, but Uncle Max's desire to go to God in his time of need that led him to a personal faith in Christ.

Prayer isn't a talisman. It's not a lucky charm. Did you know there was a time when Jesus prayed and received a "no" for an answer? It happened on the night before He gave up His life, when Jesus looked up and said, "Father, if You are willing, remove this cup from Me." He asked in agony and sorrow as He waited in the Garden. Even though the answer was no, He said, "Yet not My will, but Yours be done" (Luke 22:42).

Even if the answer to our prayers is no, we still grow closer to God when we pray. And we also grow closer as a family when we make prayer a part of our days and a constant practice in our homes.

BEDTIME BLESSINGS

Ever since our children were born, Cindy and I have prayed with them and over them at night. When Kari was only five years old, we used to wake her up in the morning with a homemade "blessing prayer."

The little singing prayer started, "Good morning, good morning, how are you today? The Lord bless you and keep you, throughout the day." It may not read like much, but this children's song sounded great when Cindy sang it. Soon this became our daughter's most requested song in the morning.

While Kari was normally a great sleeper, one time we were having trouble getting her to stay in her bed and go to sleep. We'd done a story and a prayer, a prayer and a story, water, a bathroom visit, one more story, one more glass of water, and then a last, last prayer. Finally, she was lovingly but firmly told that was it. No more games. No more stories. Time for bed. As we walked down the hall, convinced we had made our point, Kari made one last parting shot: "Good night, Mom, good night, Dad, and don't forget to bless me in the morning!"

It's hard to be angry with a kid who is asking you not to forget to pray for her in the morning, even if it's just a little song that sounds good only when Mom sings it. When you build prayer into your child's life, at mealtimes or bedtime or anytime, it makes a positive, lasting impression on him or her.

Whether it's prayer in a time of need, or prayer built into the DNA of our own or our children's daily lives, it can and does light up homes and lives.

We are living in a time when our prayers need to

convey our need for God. One of the best verses that accomplishes that is 2 Chronicles 7:14, which says, "And [if] My people who are called by My name humble themselves and pray and seek My face and turn from their wicked ways, then I will hear from heaven, will forgive their sin and will heal their land."

Our land needs healing from within and without, and that begins with a prayerful and repentant heart. The Scriptures declare that there is an appointed time for everything—a time for every event under heaven (Ecclesiastes 3:1). I can't help but think that we are living in times that call for prayer and lots of it.

Prayer pulls a family together, a community together, and a nation together.

For now, more than ever, we need to be a people of prayer.

LIVING THE LIGHT OF HOME

I hope you've enjoyed the beautiful artwork and been challenged by the ten "word pictures" of a strong family in this book. But as I close, I'd like to draw your thoughts to another outstanding painter, Claude Monet.

Many people have heard of Monet, perhaps the most famous impressionist painter of his day. Not a "starving artist," Monet lived with his wife and children in a palatial estate in the French countryside. Even today, Monet's gardens are considered some of the most beautiful in all of Europe. It was inside those garden walls that Monet captured on canvas his beautiful, peaceful masterpieces. Yet many may be unaware that these tranquil, inspiring scenes were painted during 1913–1918 amid the pain and darkness of World War I. While Monet was in his garden painting, thousands of men were marching by his estate. And like distant thunder, nearby constant artillery and machine gun fire could be heard from where his easel would have stood. That's because his peaceful gardens were less then five miles from the terrible trenches where over one million men died in battle.

It was during that time of terror, heroism, grief, and death that Monet created his paintings of life, warmth, tranquility, and beauty. And therein lies one last lesson for those of us committed to having a strong family today. In particular, it reminds me of why I was drawn to Thomas Kinkade's paintings in the first place.

As I stood next to my wife in one of his Signature Galleries years ago, the lights were slowly dimmed in a small room, and the lighthouse (*Beacon of Hope*) we watched seemed to glow with light from the inside. The darker it became on the outside, the more the home in the painting seemed to light up from within. It was an image we wanted to become a reality in our home then—and now that's even more true.

In these dark days we live in, full of terror and war and heroism and grief, it's still possible to paint pictures of love and caring and commitment and warmth in the kitchens, rooms, hallways, and backyards of our homes. Our own masterpieces are waiting to be painted in lives lived well, where marriage vows are cherished, friendships are secured, seniors are honored, and children are raised in safety, security, and love. In fact, it's not only possible, it's essential that we choose to paint these pictures. For the light of home—the light of a home full of love and hope and caring and especially faith—is indeed an unstoppable way to push back the darkness.

Dr. John Trent
PRESIDENT, STRONGFAMILIES.COM

A SPECIAL INVITATION
TO OUR READERS

The Light of Home is not just a beautiful book. It also launches a national campaign to strengthen homes and families across our country. Our goal is to see two million families sign up as "homes of light" and become lighthouses for their neighborhoods, churches, communities, and country. We invite you to visit **www.StrongFamilies.com**, where you can sign up as a "Home of Light"; receive a free weekly E-zine filled with practical help and hope; find out about Strong Families seminars; take online premarital, marriage, and parenting courses; and even join the Strong Families Book Club.

NOTES

1. Gustave Le Bon, *The Crowd—A Study of the Popular Mind*, quoted in Roy H. Williams, "When We All Think As One" in the online *Monday Morning Memo*, September 24, 2001.

2. Associated Press article in *The Arizona Republic*, December 3, 2001, "Study Says Parents Can Dissuade Kids from Smoking," quoting from *Pediatrics*, December 2001.

3. Michael Shol and Tom Spain, eds., "Miracle on a Train," in *I'll Be Home for Christmas: The Library of Congress Revisits the Spirit of Christmas During World War II* (New York: Delacorte Press, 1999), pp. 127-310. "Miracle on a Train" was originally published as: Edward Andrusko, "Welcome Home and Merry Christmas," in *Navy Times*, March 19, 1997. Used by permission.

4. Ibid., p. 127.

5. Ibid., p. 130.

6. Ibid., p. 131.